# Gears

Chris Ollerenshaw and Pat Triggs
Photographs by Peter J Millard

## Contents

Have you looked through your old toys lately? How many of them have wheels?

There are lots of things with wheels in this toy box. Some look like things we see every day. Some look like things we've never seen. How many wheels has this toy racing car got?

Did you just think about the wheels it runs on? Did you notice that there are wheels inside the racing car as well? Can you work out what they are for?

When these wheels move, the racing car moves. They are helping it to go along. The inside wheels are called gear wheels.

3

# Wheels turning wheels

Lots of things that don't run on wheels also have gear wheels that help them to work.

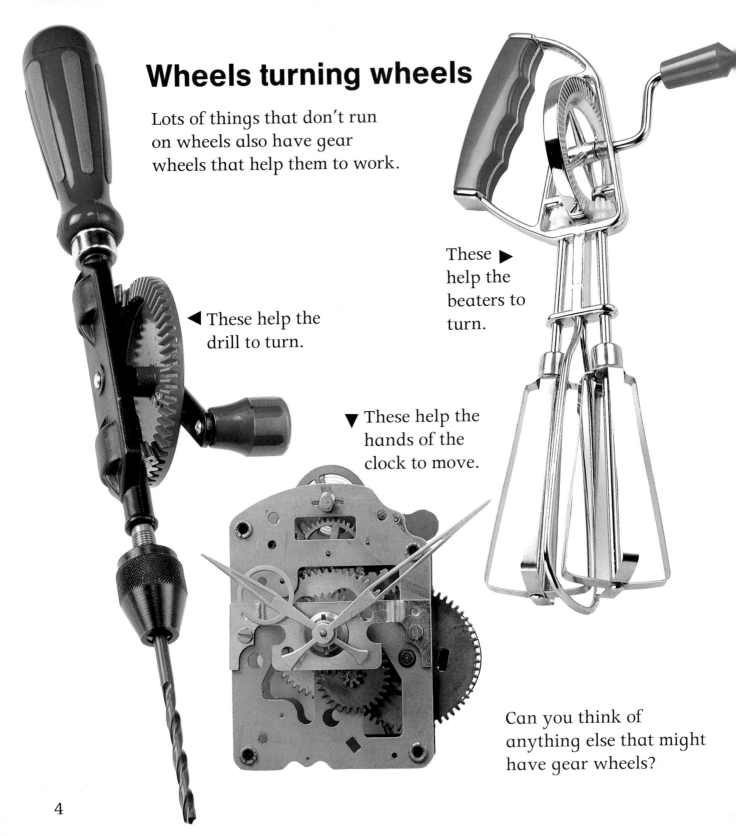

These ▶ help the beaters to turn.

◀ These help the drill to turn.

▼ These help the hands of the clock to move.

Can you think of anything else that might have gear wheels?

How does a gear wheel work? One wheel helps another wheel to turn. Look at the toy racing car again. Can you see that the wheels inside it are linked together?

Gear wheels have to be linked or they cannot work. There are different ways of linking one gear wheel with another.

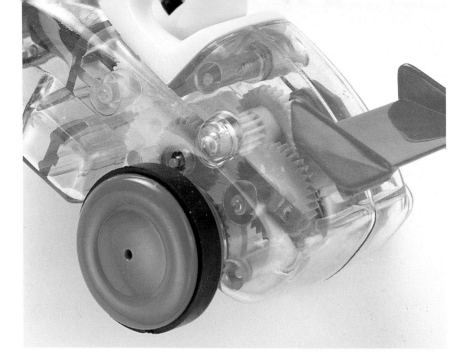

See if YOU can make one wheel turn another wheel. If this is your first try, you'll probably find that it works best if you choose:
a board with nails
two cotton reels
some rubber bands

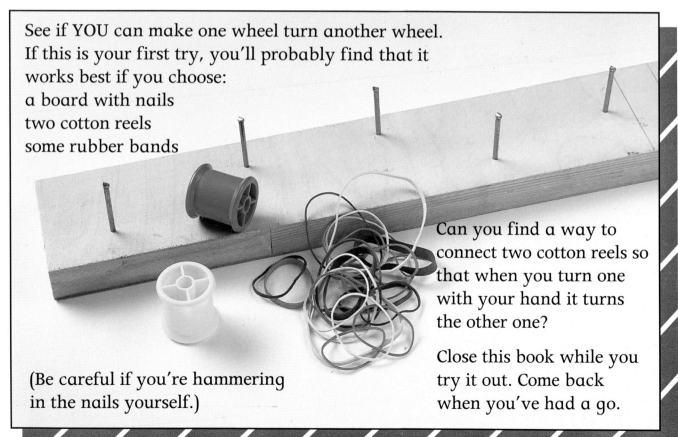

Can you find a way to connect two cotton reels so that when you turn one with your hand it turns the other one?

Close this book while you try it out. Come back when you've had a go.

(Be careful if you're hammering in the nails yourself.)

# Making links

How did you get on? Did some rubber bands turn the cotton reels better than others? Which sort of band was the best? What made it the best?

The cotton reel you are turning with your hand is called the DRIVE WHEEL. This is the one that starts the movement.

Can you see how your DRIVE WHEEL might turn more than one cotton reel? How many more cotton reels can you link together that will turn when you turn the drive wheel? Think about it and then have a try. (Hint. Try adding another rubber band every time you add another cotton reel.)

When you have got your cotton reels moving, make a drawing of them. Put arrows on your drawing to show the direction each cotton reel is moving in. (Keep your drawing. You will need it later.)

The chain of cotton reels you have just made is BELT DRIVEN. It's called belt driven because of the way the cotton reels are linked together to make them move. You used rubber bands for the belt.

# Belt drives

This model windmill works with the help of a belt drive. Not many toys are belt driven. Belts can be easily lost or broken. They can fly off or slip out of position.

Belt drives are sometimes used in everyday objects. Old vacuum cleaners have them. You can see them in the engines of some cars, too. Can you find any other toys or machines that work with the help of a belt drive? Are the belts in these machines in any way like the rubber bands that you used?

Make a collection of materials that you think would make good belts for a belt drive. How are the materials you have chosen like each other? What would be the MOST important things to look out for in any material you were going to use for a belt drive? Thinking about exactly what each material will do will help you decide whether it will make a suitable belt.

# Linking wheels

This photograph was taken at a working farm museum. It shows a belt drive linking a traction engine (on the right of the picture) with a machine for threshing corn.

The machinery was in use a hundred years ago. Before it was invented people had to beat the ears of corn on a hard floor to get the grain to fall out. That took a long time and was very tiring.

On modern farms, combine harvesters do the jobs that used to be done by traction engines and threshing machines. They also do other jobs like cutting and binding. Combine harvesters have wheels inside them to help them work, but the wheels are not linked by belts.

What other ways are there of linking wheels to make gears? Look again at the toy racing car, the drill and the beater. And look at these pictures of the gears inside a crane (above) and on a canal lock (left). Can you see how the gears on these machines touch each other directly?

# Wheels that touch

Can you make one wheel turn another wheel which is touching it?

Collect some lids. Start by pinning two lids to a piece of card so that one is just touching the other. Turn one and see what happens.

Now collect a selection of materials. Cut strips that will fit around the edges of the lids. See if there is a difference in the way the lids turn as you try out each material.

Do any of the materials cause the lids to slip as they turn so that it is hard for one to turn the other? Which materials allow the lids to get a good grip on each other and turn easily?

# Gear wheels have teeth

Did you choose smooth lids or lids with rough or ridged edges? Did you find that some lids gripped each other and turned more easily than others?

The best surface is one that allows the wheels to lock together as they turn. Try it out.

Collect some deep-sided lids and some corrugated paper strips. Fix the strips to the lids and test how well they turn each other.

If you have squashed the ridges in the paper or made a lumpy join your lids may not be turning very well.

Gear wheels usually have teeth cut into them, like these. The teeth work like the ridges in the corrugated paper. If the teeth are damaged the gear wheels don't work properly.

15

# Connections and directions

Look again at your wheels that touch each other. Which direction are they moving in? Make a picture of them and mark the direction with arrows.

Are these wheels moving in the same directions as the ones you connected by belt drive? (Check with your drawing of the cotton reels.) Wheels move in different directions depending on how they are connected to each other.

Now make another belt drive with cotton reels, but this time twist the band so that it is crossed over between the cotton reels. Turn the drive wheel. What happens? Make another picture to show which way the reels turn. Now you have three diagrams that show your different sets of wheels turning. What do you notice?

## Different sizes, different speeds?

Look again at the threshing machine and the traction engine. The big drive wheel on the traction engine is connected by a belt to the smaller wheel on the threshing machine.

What difference do you think it makes when a large wheel is linked to a smaller wheel?

If you want to find out, try this: collect two different sized jar lids and fix them with paper fasteners to a piece of cardboard or an old cereal box. Make sure that you put the fasteners through the exact centre of each lid. Use rubber bands to make one wheel turn another. Are both wheels turning at the same speed?

To find out, make a small mark on the edge of each lid. Line up your marks with a start line on your box. Make the larger lid the drive wheel. Turn it once until the mark is back at your start line. How many times did the mark on the smaller wheel pass the start line?

Now make the smaller lid the drive wheel. Turn it once. What has happened to the mark on the larger wheel?

# What have you found out?

Gear wheels help to make things move. Gear wheels can move in different directions depending on how they are connected. Gear wheels can be different sizes. Gear wheels which are different sizes turn a different number of times.

Because of this, we can use gears to make work easier. Remember the way the belt driven wheels helped to thresh the corn?

This huge Ferris wheel (in the main picture) is being moved by the effort of turning the smaller wheels (in the smaller picture).

Here are two kitchen whisks. Which of them do you think will help you to whip an egg white faster?

Try it out. How will you make it a fair test?

# Making work easier

How did you get on? Of course, the rotary whisk was faster – and it didn't make your arm ache as much either. Why did it work better? Look again at what happened.

The simple hand whisk moves as fast as your hand moves. The rotary whisk beats faster than your hand because it has gears.

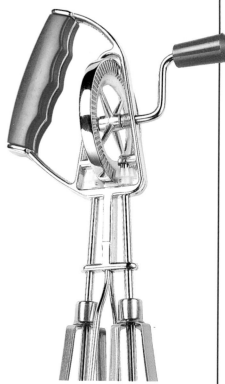

When your hand turned the large drive wheel once, the smaller wheels like these white plastic ones turned lots of times. So the egg white got beaten faster and you didn't have to work so hard.

What else have you found out about gears?

We can use them to move heavy loads.    We can use them to save time.

All gears make work easier.
Can you find out how gears help a bicycle like this one to work?

# Flat and upright gears

There's a helicopter in the toy box. To make the blades turn you have to push the helicopter along the ground.

The wheels on the helicopter are connected to the blades by gears.

Did you notice that one gear wheel is upright and the other is flat?

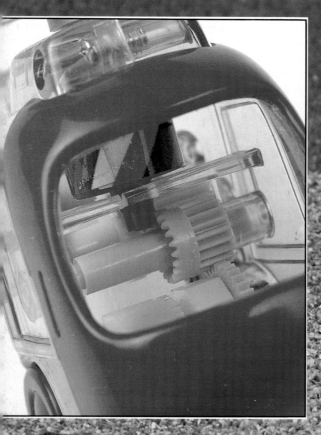

See if you can make a flat or horizontal gear turn an upright or vertical gear wheel. The trick is to get the teeth of the gears in the right place to interlock.

Can you see how the gear wheels in this water mill turn each other? Being able to turn the movement from vertical to horizontal is useful. Look back at the pictures of the rotary whisk and the drill.

# Using gears safely

Lots of machines have gears which are closed in to keep them safe from damage and us safe from injury.

See if you can put some gears inside a box.
Here are some ideas to help you.

You can use this mechanism to make a roundabout or a helicopter or a machine that you've designed yourself.

# Make a model helicopter

The blueprint on pages 30 and 31 of this book will help you to make a model helicopter like this one. Use the plans to build the outside shell. You can then design and make the gears to put inside and make it work. Your gears can be made from junk or card and wood. Just make sure they will fit inside your model!

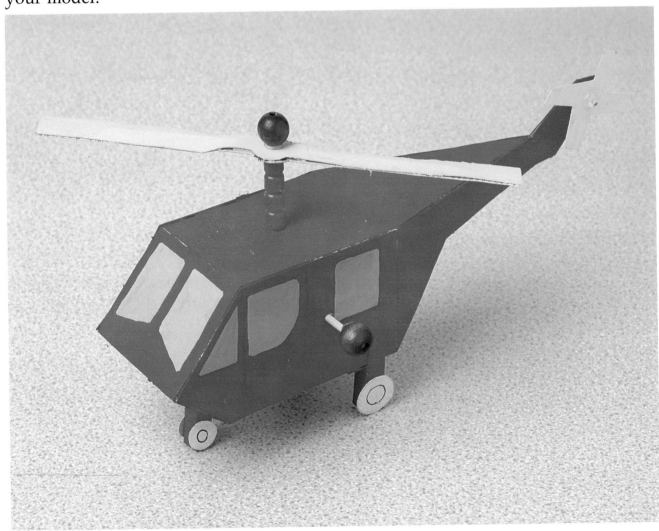

# Index

This paperback edition published 1999
by A & C Black (Publishers) Limited
35 Bedford Row, London, WC1R 4JH.

First published in hardback 1991.

Text © 1991 Chris Ollerenshaw and Pat Triggs
All photographs © Peter J Millard except pg 10t,
18, 23 Acton Scott Working Farm Museum; pg 10b
Farmer's Weekly; pg 11t Bristol Industrial Museum
(Tony Clancey); pg 11b British Waterways; pg 20, 23
John Heinrich; pg 26 Beamish

ISBN 0-7136-5229-2

Illustrations by David Ollerenshaw.

A CIP catalogue record for this book
is available from the British Library.

Filmset by August Filmsetting, Haydock, St Helens.
Printed in Belgium by Proost International Book
Production.

Acknowledgments

The photographer, authors and publishers would
like to thank the following people whose help and
co-operation made this book possible: Simone,
Nicola, Gehaan, Danny, Arthur, Ashton and the
staff and pupils at Avondale Park Primary School,
Royal Borough of Kensington and Chelsea.

# Helicopter

Make and fit gears so that you can work the rotor blade by turning a handle on the side of the model.

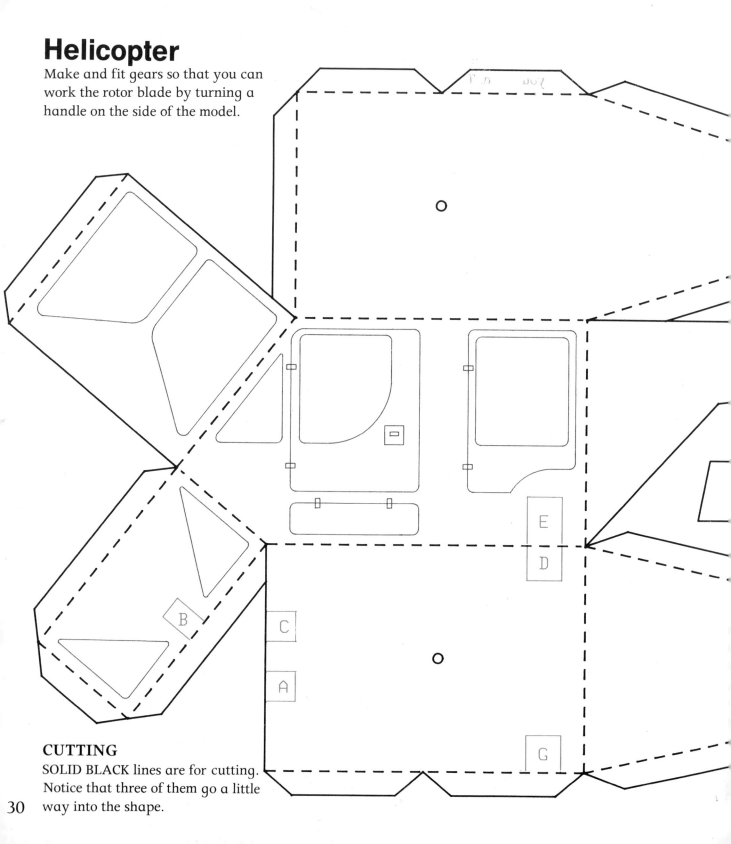

## CUTTING

SOLID BLACK lines are for cutting. Notice that three of them go a little way into the shape.

30

## TRACING

Trace the plan onto card before you begin. Trace the left side of the blueprint first. Next, position one vertical blue line on top of the other. Then continue tracing. Trace dotted lines very carefully, especially where they begin and end. Two of them look straight at first – but they're not!

## CONSTRUCTION

One side of the helicopter has been left out to make fitting the gears easier. Make up the model, then trace and cut out the missing side when you need it.

## FOLDING

BLACK DOTTED lines are for folding. Score before you fold. Use a ruler and a small screwdriver.

## GLUEING

Glue one or two tabs at a time.

## DECORATING

RED LINES suggest ideas for decoration (look back at the picture of the model helicopter on page 28).

TAIL ROTOR

## ROTOR BLADE

You may need thicker card for this.

*How to fold the legs*

## UNDERCARRIAGE

The model stands on the legs. Match the letters when glueing the tabs to the model. The wheels are for effect only.

A   B   C

D   E

F   G

*A David Ollerenshaw design*

NOSE LEG

REAR LEGS

31

# Notes for teachers and parents

Each title in this series promotes investigation as a way of learning about science and being scientific. Children are invited to try things out and think things through for themselves. It's very important for the children to handle the materials mentioned in the books, as only by making their own scientific explorations can they construct an explanation that works for them.

Each Toybox Science book is structured so that it follows a planned cycle of learning. At the **orientation** stage, with a starting point which mixes familiar and unfamiliar materials, children draw on their previous experience to organise their ideas. **Exploration** encourages clarification and refining of ideas and leads to **investigation**. At this stage children are testing and comparing, a process which leads to developing, restructuring and replacing ideas. **Reviewing** is an important part of this stage and can occur at the end or throughout as appropriate. Children discuss what they have found out and draw conclusions, perhaps using recorded data. Finally, open-ended problems provide opportunities for **application** of acquired knowledge and skills.

In writing these books we drew on our practical experience of this cycle to select and sequence activities, to frame questions, to make strategic decisions about when to provide information and introduce specialized vocabulary, when to summarise and suggest recording. The use of real world applications and the introduction of a historical perspective are to encourage the linkage of ideas.

The **blueprint** at the end of each book encourages children to apply their learning in a new situation. There is no right answer to how to get the inside mechanism to work; the problem could be solved in any number of ways and children should be left to find their own.

**The national curriculum**: the first four books in the series are concerned with energy, forces and the nature of materials explored within an overall notion of movement and how things work.

### GEARS

Gears are part of a machine that makes work easier by controlling movement (kinetic) energy. Force is involved because it can make things move faster, move slower or change direction. The range of materials used in the making of gears in the book explores ideas about the different properties that makes them more or less suitable for different purposes. There are openings for developing ideas about friction.

### Resources

Children working with this book will be best supported by:

- A collection of assorted materials similar to those mentioned in the book.
- A resource box of tools and basics like paper fasteners, rubber bands, etc and everyday junk materials (to be stored and labelled to allow children to access them independently).
- The availability of construction kits collections of toys and real world objects similar to those mentioned in the book.
- Books and pictures related to the topic of the book to support enquiry and investigation.
- Visits to places where they can see real world applications, current and historical.